DON'T GET OUTWORKED

THE GUIDE TO UNLEASHING YOUR FULL POTENTIAL

DARREN TAYLOR

Don't Get Outworked

Copyright © 2017 by Darren Taylor

For information contact : Darren Taylor
http://dontgetoutworked.com

Cover design by Daniel Gensollen
ISBN: 978-0-9987392-0-5

First Edition: April 2017

10 9 8 7 6 5 4 3 2 1

Dedication

To all those who are pushing toward a dream, a goal, or a desire. This book is for you.

Contents

INTRODUCTION: Stop Getting Outworked

"People see all of the accomplishments but little do they know it requires a tremendous amount of sacrifice, sleepless nights, and hard work. You cannot put stipulations on what you will or won't do when you are pursuing a goal. It requires an attitude geared towards doing whatever it takes to get there. "

Darren Taylor

Whether it was the book cover, the catchy title, or a friend, something brought you to this very moment, holding this book in your hands, and reading these very words from the page. Let me tell you something. This book is not for the weak-minded.

This is not the book for someone who just "kind of" wants to be successful. Don't even bother reading this book if you want to be average. You've already wasted enough time settling for an average life, with average goals. You can put this book down and continue being mediocre, just know this one thing; you WILL get outworked.

For those of you who are ready to begin this life altering journey, don't be discouraged by your current situation. We all have to start somewhere. There is nothing wrong with living an average life. There's a difference between living average and dying average.

If you're living average, you still have time to make a change. You are a living, breathing machine that is well-equipped to do anything you set your mind to.

Dying average and not pursuing your goals means that you took all of your time, potential, and intellect for granted.

Don't Settle For Good

"The graveyard is the richest place on earth, because it is here that you will find all the hopes and dreams that were never fulfilled, the books that were never written, the songs that were never sung, the inventions that were never shared, the cures that were never discovered, all because someone was too afraid to take that first step, keep with the problem, or determined to carry our their dream." -

Les Brown

We are all capable of being great, but few of us are willing to do what it takes. Some of us settle for the good things we have instead of taking a leap of faith to receive the great things ahead.

Don't be the person who always says, "Well, I wish I woulda... but..."

Don't be someone who lets their excuses hold them back.

When I die I want to be a liability and not an asset to the grave

Become an Expert Problem Solver

Become an expert problem solver. When the going gets tough, take the "tough", solve the problem, and keep going.

Some problems are complex with no simple solution, but never underestimate the power of your mind. Approach every situation with a positive attitude no matter how trying it may be.

For an example, let's say that you have a 2-hour commute to work every morning that you absolutely hate. By the time you get to work you are so irritated that you treat everyone around you badly.

You disperse an abundance of negativity each day you come in the doors. Throughout the day, you are less productive because you are trapped in your office, suffocating in negativity.

The most obvious solution to this problem would be to relocate closer to your job, right? Right. That is, if you have the complete freedom to do so. My guess is that you probably can't get up and move whenever you please.

What you can do is make use of your commute. We spend a lot of time in our vehicles or on public transportation. Put this time to use for you. Start listening to audiobooks, motivational speeches, or scriptures while you're driving.

Use this idle time to expand your mind. Make the most of your commute. This is a great way to mentally prepare yourself for a successful day. It's just that simple. If you can change the way you perceive a situation, you can change the way you approach it.

Work to Better Yourself

When you rid your mind of the words "I can't", when you stand up and say, "Fuck the excuses!" and when you walk away from all the negativity that haunts you, this is your time to grind. From now on, when you walk into a room, look at it as an opportunity to inspire or to be inspired.

You should be working so hard to better yourself that people see you and are inspired to go after all they've ever wanted. Your positive approach to all situations will shine and people will notice.

There's also the potential of meeting a like-minded individual that may have wisdom to share with you. Walk into a room with the mindset that no one will outwork you. That winning attitude alone will be noticed and respected. You will reap an abundance of benefits once you decide to never be outworked.

It won't be easy. When you get tired and give up, know that someone somewhere is working on the exact same idea that you are, and they are outworking you. Know that when you find reasons to stop your efforts, you are letting your excuses outwork you.

Become Obsessed With Your Goal

When I have a goal, I become completely obsessed with it. Each and everything I do revolves around that goal. I sacrifice all distractions. I sacrifice my sleep when needed. I read my goals, and see my goals every single morning, afternoon, and night. I am a competitor and my biggest competition is yesterday's self.

Each day I strive to be better than I was the day before, no matter what it takes. "Don't Get Outworked" is an impenetrable mindset that will nearly guarantee your success in anything you put your mind to. This book will give you the blueprint to tap into this mindset.

I will share tips, tools, and routines that I have personally applied to my life. This mindset has helped me to achieve every goal I set for myself. It can do the same thing for you.

CHAPTER 1: Don't Let Me Outwork You!

"The road to success is always paved with consistent hard work.

Outwork your competitors, be authentic, and above all else...chase your greatness!"

Dwayne "The Rock" Johnson

I will never forgot the day I resigned from my last job several years ago. I was a Loss Mitigation Negotiator for one of the top mortgage companies. I hated every bit of waking up, fighting traffic just to get to a place that I hated and wasn't appreciated.

The day I resigned from my job I told my boss that I would rather work in a warehouse or mow lawns than be in a negative environment that drained me and didn't appreciate hard work.

I have always been confident in my work ethic and the day I left my job was when I truly embraced the "Don't get outworked" mentality. Applying that mentality gave me the edge to put myself in a position to be my own boss.

Let's be real, many of us hate our 9-5's. Most people are doing things in life that they are not passionate about. We could create a whole list of things we would rather do. If we can think of even one thing we'd rather do, why don't we?

You have the power to create the life you want. All you have to do is use your power. You have to possess a strong belief system in which you know that you are capable of anything you put your mind to. You have a passion. You have a talent. You have a burning desire. The question is...what are you going to do with it?

Power in Holy Spirit

Follow Your Passion

Build your life around your passion. Follow your passion and the profit will follow. Quit working for someone who is using your time to help pursue their dreams, while yours are slowly being pushed further and further away.

Many people are not in a position where they can walk away from their jobs today and be financially stable. That's okay!

You're going to have to make the necessary sacrifices. Look at your daily routine and assess each thing you do. Decide what is adding value and what is deducting value. Sacrifice all of the things that are hindering you from taking the first step.

If you like to go out to happy hour with your co-workers at the end of your day, sacrifice that time and dedicate it to your destiny. Instead of going out to happy hour, go to work on drawing your business plan or sharpening your craft.

Think of it as if you are now juggling two full-time jobs, except your whole life depends on one of them. The way you spend your leisure time will decide what you can accomplish.

Any major level of achievement is the direct result of your work ethic. You can watch your vision come to life or you can live visualizing the life you always wanted.

It will haunt you if you keep your vision trapped inside your head. When you have an idea, it should never be taken for granted. Ideas are blessings. They are suggestions that are brought to our attention for a reason. Every great thing started as a mere idea.

Focus Your Vision

Turn your ideas into visions. Write your vision down on a piece of paper, and read it everyday. This will ensure that your vision is on the forefront of your mind. That's just the first step.

Before you know it, you will be seeing and hearing things throughout your day that add to your vision. Write all of those down as well.

You will begin to attract relevant people and relevant thoughts because you will be so engulfed in your vision. Now I encourage you to set relevant goals.

Stay obedient to your vision. Be realistic, set goals that are achievable.

That doesn't mean set goals that you perceive as easy. Challenge yourself. Give yourself something to strive toward. This will help you stay motivated.

Start today and write out five short term and five long term goals.

I literally view my goals throughout the day on my steering wheel in my vehicle. I set reminders on my phone.

I truly believe you should see your goals throughout the day as a constant reminder to avoid anything that is not helping you achieve them.

We live in a world full of distractions and it is very important not to give your attention to things that have nothing to do with your goals.

There is no greater feeling than the satisfaction you get from achieving a goal you've set for yourself. Especially when you had to work hard for it. Even if you doubted yourself initially, you made the decision to do something.

Achieving that goal will help you prove to yourself that you are capable of achieving anything you set your mind to doing, and it will reinforce your ability to believe that you are capable of great things.

Assess Your Work Ethic

You have a vision. You have goals that you've set because you want your vision to become a reality. This is the easiest part. This is the part that anyone and everyone can do.

Your work ethic is what will set you apart from everyone else who has a vision and goals. Expect more from yourself and put all of your focus on the outcome instead of the process it takes reaching your goal.

Do you want to be good or great? When you get tired, do you quit or do you keep working? When you have negativity in your life, do you keep dwelling in it, or do you cut it loose? When you leave your 9-5, do you make time for your vision or do you relax like you're already rich?

These are questions you should ask yourself in order to assess your current work ethic. The answers to these questions will decide whether you will be outworked or not.

There are nearly 7.5 billion people on this planet. Odds are that you aren't the only one with your vision or your idea.

If you have a new innovative idea, you need to feel a sense of urgency. At any moment one of the 7.5 billion of us could take that idea right up from under you.

You have to outwork your competition to be the best. Just imagine someone somewhere coming for what is yours.

This brilliant idea that is going to add value to

your life and the lives of others. They want it badly, but you want must want it even more than they do.

Tell yourself that you are willing to do whatever it takes to be great. Tell yourself you will never be outworked.

Be The First In and The Last Out

This is the mindset that I have lived by for many years. I use it to keep me motivated, but more importantly, I use it to motivate others around me.

If you know me well, I'm sure you've gotten a message from me early in the morning or late at night that says, "Don't let me outwork you!"

I use that myself as a constant reminder to people around me that if you want something badly enough, you have to work for it. I am always the first person in the office and the last person to leave the office. To be successful, you have to put in those extra hours.

One person that I have always been inspired by is Bill Gates. I admire his work ethic. He worked 16 hours a day all the time when he was starting his company.

I'd also note that Bill Gates said that he never took a day off in his twenties. His relentless work ethic and passion about his craft has made him the second richest man in the world.

I would like to also mention how Mark Cuban went seven years straight without a vacation while building his business. Every major level of success is going to come with a price.

Both of these very successful men made huge sacrifices that eventually paid off tremendously. It takes years of sacrifice, dedication, and discipline to reach that level of success.

You must be prepared to sacrifice weeks, months, or even years when pursuing your passion. Become a master of your craft and also know that you cannot achieve anything great without paying a price.

Know that there will be competitors out there that will want to take what you have. But the most important thing about competing is to always compete with yourself first.

You are your biggest competition. Don't strive to be better than the successful people you see on TV and social media. Strive to be better than the person you were the day before. Before you know it, you'll look back a year from now thinking, "Wow! Look how far I have come."

Build Your Belief System

It's your belief system that will keep you holding

on when you feel like letting go. You must believe that you can accomplish any task.

When thinking about your goals and your vision, visualize that you have already accomplished what you set out to do.

Create affirmations that you can recite throughout the day to maximize your beliefs that you ARE the successful person you want to be. At the end of the day, everything boils down to a decision.

Believe in your vision and capitalize on it. Decide who you want to be. Write down how you plan to become that person.

Tell yourself that you are that person. Once you believe in yourself, others will see it in you and you will find yourself in a position to truly achieve greatness.

Your beliefs will either make you or break you. A strong belief system is often the difference between those who give up and those who succeed.

CHAPTER 2: I've Come A Long Way!

"Sometimes, we use the past to justify our current decision-making, and that's the reason we don't want to let go...- those memories justify everything for you...when you're unable to let go, that becomes a part of your 'story' and works against you- holding you back"

Tony Robbins

Many of you may be questioning my credibility. I'm giving you a lists of do's and don'ts, telling you what I believe your mindset should be, and you may be thinking, "this guy is crazy."

It's possible you think my expectations for you are unrealistic. Maybe you think I'm full of shit!

I can understand. I'm going to share my story just so you can see that I really do understand your situation.

My childhood home in Dalworth

Where I Started

I grew up in a small town just outside of Dallas, TX called Dalworth. It's the type of town where you are either in school, playing sports, or getting into trouble. As a child in Dalworth, there wasn't much to keep the kids busy other than playing outside. That is, for most kids.

I started my own business at eight years of age. Sounds crazy, I know, but I felt that I didn't have any other choice. My mother was addicted to crack-cocaine and my father was in prison.

My grandfather repaired and sold lawn mowers to the people who lived in the neighborhood. Seeing my grandfather work and get money in return, I figured I could do the same thing.

At my young age, about the only thing I could think of doing to make money was mowing lawns in the summer and raking leaves in the Fall.

I went door-to-door asking all of my neighbors if they would let me mow their lawns. The community responded well to my request and, before you knew it, I had approximately 20 clients.

I can remember some of them already had a professional lawn care service mowing their lawns but they would let me come by and cut over their freshly cut lawn just to support my business.

People saw that while all of the other kids were playing, I was working. I had already decided I would not be outworked at a very young young age.

Chasing Easy Money

Unfortunately, in small towns like Dalworth, selling drugs is all too common. When I got a bit older, I added that to my list of hustles, as did almost all of the people that I surrounded myself with.

I was fortunate enough to never get caught up with it while I was in high school, but I saw so many who did.

Many of the people I knew and were friends with growing up were sent to jail or prison for the same exact things I was doing. I never got caught, and I took that for granted. After graduating high school, I was blessed to go to college.

Kicked Out For Drug Possession

You're probably thinking that I went to a great school and got my degree. That's another thing I took for granted. I let my old, small town ways follow me into my "new" life.

I thought that graduating high school and going to college would be enough. I settled for the good things I had, when I should have been striving for the greater things ahead.

I was kicked out of college my freshman year for the possession of marijuana. I was so disappointed in myself. There I was, a young man who has an addict for a mother, a felon for a father, and I just got kicked out school for drug possession.

I was living a textbook example of what happens to average people who want to live average lives. I was on a path that would surely send me exactly where my father was. It didn't matter how hard I worked if my mind wasn't in the right place.

I learned an important lesson from that experience. Making money is good, and if making more money is your goal, that's great. But you can't only see green. Don't ignore the red flags.

You have to see the good and the bad. If you're willing to get money any and every way, you may need to reevaluate. You have to make sure you aren't doing anything to hinder your success.

The Struggle To Find Work

After that, it was nearly impossible to find a job where I could make even decent money. With my background, hard labor jobs were all I could find.

I would spend my days working my ass off for minimum wage. That time period of my life was one of the most frustrating.

I share all of this to say, "Don't be discouraged."

We all go through hardships that will either make us or break us.

If that's your story currently, know that you can change your future based upon the decisions you make today.

For me personally, I have always been an entrepreneur. I felt that I had no other choice. I knew that working minimum wage would not lead me to a life that I wanted.

Fast Forward To Today

Today, my life is extremely different. I have two amazing sons that keep me motivated to give them a life that I never had growing up. I could have used my past as an excuse not to get anywhere in life.

Instead, I have let those experiences and challenges I faced play a huge role in everything that I ever accomplished. I have always used my past as a reminder of the importance of always working hard.

Over the years, I have established a generous amount of people who look to me for advice and inspiration. This didn't happen by accident. It happened because I made a decision that I was not going to be average.

I was not going to live an average life, or get caught in the mistakes of my parents. I was not going to be outworked.

I have been granted multiple opportunities to appear on several magazine covers, as well as some fitness features. But this doesn't make me any different from you. This doesn't make me better or more accomplished.

I'm on the mission of not being outworked just like you. Everything I say to you, I use in my own everyday life.

You can also have that kind of life. All you have to do is make that same decision that you are not going to be outworked ever again. You are not going to be average. You are going to rise above all of that and you are going to succeed.

You are not going to use your past as an excuse as to why you can't do great things. You are going to accomplish the great things that are meant for you to do.

CHAPTER 3: Never Settle For Average

"There's no talent here, this is hard work...This is an obsession.

Talent does not exist, we are all equals as human beings. You could be anyone if you put in the time. You will reach the top, and that's that.

I am not talented, I am obsessed."

Conor McGregor

Average is so easy. Average requires nothing of you. You don't have to stand out or do anything different than the rest of the crowd.

Average doesn't challenge you, it doesn't risk anything, and it certainly doesn't cost you anything. Average is just comfortable. If it isn't obvious already, average is nothing to strive for, and worse, there are subtle dangers to aiming for average.

Average People Don't Achieve Great Things

The first danger to being average is that you will never truly achieve what you were born to achieve. You will never be great because, by definition, you're just average. You will never, ever make the difference that you were born to make because you just settled.

The people who need you for guidance and leadership will never find you because you are so busy blending in with the crowd that you've gotten lost in this boring sea of average. They will lose their way because you lacked the courage to seek and claim your innate greatness, a greatness each and every human being has within themselves if they only choose to look for it.

It doesn't matter what you believe. You were born

for greatness. There has never, in all of history, been another you, nor will there ever be another you. No one else in time or space will ever have your unique combination of life experience, genetic inheritance, skills, talents, knowledge, and gifts all wrapped into one.

You are the only human in all of the world who can do what you were born to do. You're a unique opportunity unleashed in the world for a singular purpose. You have a responsibility to fulfill that role. If you've found that purpose, you have zero excuses for not acting upon it.

Sure, you can stand idly by and allow others to attempt your calling, but they will not be able to execute it the way you would or as well as you could. Their efforts will be good, but good is not great.

You are the person best suited to do it, so why aren't you?

This is why it is so important that you commit yourself not to get outworked by your inferiors. Other people may wander into the notion that they can do whatever you're doing, they imitate by nature, but only you will know that you can do it better.

It is up to you to bring that greatness to what would otherwise just be good. Don't settle for good, good is just average.

An Average Life Isn't A Joyful Life

A second danger to living an average life is that an average life won't bring you joy. That isn't to say you won't experience happiness sometimes. Happiness and joy are not the same things.

Happiness is an emotional response to a change in your circumstances. That's why it doesn't last. Joy only comes when you're living up to your highest potential in life by stepping into your purpose and living it.

When you have found joy, that doesn't go away no matter what's happening in your life. Joy is an inner certainty that you are on the right path and that the path you are walking is going to take you good places even if you have to go through dark times to get there.

Until you find that purpose and start living it, though, you're going to struggle with bouts of depression. Depression gets you asking questions like, "What's the point of life?" and "Why does it matter that I'm here?" so that you will eventually go looking for the answers.

Once you have found your purpose, depression will be there every time you leave it behind to make sure that you're not satisfied with life until you go back and commit to that purpose wholeheartedly.

You don't have to believe what I'm saying. There are plenty of studies out there about the difference in life between those who find and live their purpose and those who don't.

Having a purpose in life reduces the risk of mortality across your lifetime. Those with a purpose sleep better, feel better, are healthier, and enjoy life more than their non-purpose driven counterparts.

Living your purpose and fulfilling your highest potential is what will bring you to life and make you feel excited about each new day. When you are living your life doing the thing that you were born to do and sharing that greatness with other people, you will feel alive in a way you have never felt alive before.

You will know that you could do this work all day every day without stopping. In fact, you wouldn't want to stop. It's just a part of who you already are.Imagine waking up and you don't even need an alarm clock because you can't wait to get out there and get to work doing what brings you joy to do!

Imagine what your life would be like if you could live every single day excited, fulfilled, and eager to meet the challenges. This is what your life will begin to look like the moment you commit to finding and living your greatness. This is what will come from deciding that you will never again be outworked.

The Battle For Greatness

Nobody has greatness handed to them. It's a battle all the way.

Dwayne "The Rock" Johnson is one of wrestling's most famous superstars. He has appeared in Hollywood movies, on Saturday Night Live, and in wrestling venues all over the United States. However, he wasn't born into greatness. It came as a result of an uphill battle.

> "I'm always asked,
> 'What's the secret to success?'
>
> But there are no secrets.
>
> Be humble. Be hungry.
> And always be the hardest worker in the room."
>
> Dwayne "The Rock" Johnson

He was born to a Samoan mother and black Nova Scotian WWE Hall of Fame Wrestling Star Rocky Johnson. Rocky moved his growing family from town to town, place to place, always following the paychecks offered to him in whatever jobs he could find.

As a result, Dwayne attended schools in New Zealand, parts of Canada, Hawaii, Texas, and Pennsylvania while he was growing up. No matter where he went, though, he always made a name for himself in sports whether it was track and field, wrestling, or football.

A host of division 1 colleges pursued him, offering athletic scholarships, and eventually he chose to play for the University of Miami in 1991. In 1992 after suffering a serious injury, he was replaced by Warren Sapp, who wound up becoming an NFL Hall of Fame recipient.

After graduating in 1995, Johnson signed a three year deal with a Canadian football team, but was cut from the team just two months later.

He returned home with $7 to his name and struggled with depression for weeks. Eventually, he decided to follow his father, grandfather, and cousin into the professional wrestling circuit.

His father discouraged him because he knew how hard it was to make it in that profession and he wanted more for his son than he'd experienced himself.

He made his debut in the USWA under the name Flex Kavanagh and won the tag team championship with Brett sawyer. He joined the WWE in 1996 as Rocky Maivia.

His entrance didn't meet with much success until after he joined a group called the "Nation of Domination" and turned 'heel' - a wrestling term for the bad guys who break the rules and whom crowds love to hate.

After taking over leadership of the Nation, Rocky began developing the persona of "The Rock". It was as The Rock that he began his climb to fame.

When the Nation split, The Rock joined a group of elite wrestlers known as "The Corporation" and began a feud with one of the top stars of the day - "Stone Cold" Steve Austin.

That feud launched him to fame and showcased his exceptional flair for the dramatic. It was this dramatic ability that would attract the attention of Saturday Night Live and, eventually, Hollywood.

The Truth About You

You weren't born into easy circumstances. You may have been born to a drug addicted mother, like

I was, or to parents who were extremely mentally unhealthy. Maybe you had an absentee father like I did.

There is a reason why you were put into that situation from the beginning. Those hardships are the crucible in which great leaders are tested and refined.

Look around you. Is there any doubt that there is a lack of leadership in our country and the world?

Great leaders don't wait for someone else to solve problems. They spot the problems that need solving and they go out and they find or create the solutions that will solve them. They are proactive, taking steps to make things happen, rather than waiting for things to happen to them.

You were born to be a leader, but up until now you have not been living up to your potential. You have been letting yourself be led around by life.

You have been drifting in the sea of average waiting for someone to notice you, spot your potential, and help you make something of it.

Let me tell you a secret: as long as you are average, you will never be noticed. You will look too much like everyone else to stand out in a crowd.

Stop Trying So Hard to Fit In

Average people fit in with the crowd. If you want to stop being average, you're going to have to stop trying so hard to fit in and take pride in standing out from the crowd. You're going to have to stop being a follower and start taking the lead.

Leaders can't afford to fit in or blend in with the rest of everybody else. They have to stand out so that the people who need them can find them

Blending in and fitting in feels good. It is comfortable. It is easy. It gains you acceptance and it earns you approval. Nobody's threatened by someone who is average. Nobody is challenged by someone who is average.

Standing out from the crowd gets you challenged, questioned, and looked at as if you were an odd ball. You're treated differently, sometimes ridiculed, and often misunderstood. It takes courage to be willing to stand in your own greatness and own it.

When you don't fit in with everyone else, you can feel as if there's something wrong with you. However, nothing is further from the truth. There's nothing wrong with you being radically different.

It's what you were born to be. You are not created to blend in or fit in or be like everyone else. You were created to serve a specific, unique purpose that you and only you can fulfill.

Every future leader must eventually learn how to

stand on his or her own two feet. They must learn to push against the crowd and to become self-sufficient.

It's a tough lesson to learn, but those who don't learn it get swept away by the tide of popular opinion. They aren't strong enough to serve the purpose of standing up for what's right when no one else has the strength or the willpower to do it.

True leaders have to be able to stand against the crowd when it's headed the wrong direction and speak up in defense of the defenseless even when they're being shouted down by others.

You aren't called to be a follower. You're called to be a leader. That's why you're reading this book.

A Portrait of Success

In an article on success printed in the Huffington post, they listed qualities that successful people have that other people don't. Look at these qualities and think about which of these you already have and which you need to develop.

1. Successful people don't accept rules until they understand the reasons.

2. They seek the truth and are willing to challenge conventional wisdom.

3. They believe in the impossible and when

people tell them they can't do it, they let that motivate them instead of letting it discourage them.

4. They embrace failure and recognize it as the fastest path to success.

5. They know themselves and their purpose and they are relentless in pursuing it.

6. They constantly check themselves to be sure they are staying in alignment with their purpose and they take corrective action as soon as they notice a problem.

7. When they notice that something needs to be done, they take ownership over getting it done and don't wait for other people to take care of it.

8. They set long-term and short-term goals and refuse to let life get in the way of the goals they set.

9. They are confident in themselves and in what they commit to doing.

10. They use time well and are optimistic about

the future because they know they can make good things happen for themselves.

11. They don't just welcome challenges, they actively seek them out and look for ways to push themselves to the next level.

12. They are hyperfocused on getting done what needs to be done and they don't allow themselves to be distracted.

It's Time To Step Up

You picked up this book for a reason. You're reading it for a reason. The reason for it is this: something inside you is ready to change. Something inside you is telling you it is time to step out of the shadows and stop trying to fit in and step into the spotlight so you can be seen. The world needs you. It's about time you stepped up.

You may be overwhelmed by the amount of problems there are in the world and the thought of leading anyone may scare you.

What if you fail them? What if you lead them in the wrong direction? What if they follow you and blame you for where they end up as a result?

It's true. Leadership is a giant responsibility. It is

one you have been avoiding your whole life because you didn't feel worthy. However, it's time to stop kidding yourself about who you are and what you are capable of doing.

You have so much more inside of you than you've ever dared to let people see, but it's time to change that. This is why I'm here to help you.

Believe In Yourself

Your life may be rampant with doubt—doubt from your parents, from your friends, from your classmates, from your coworkers, from every realm of life. You may have been told that you were good for nothing, or that your disabilities meant that you could never do anything meaningful, or that you weren't good enough for any reason in particular whether legitimate or not. You may have been told you were a mistake, an accident, or that you shouldn't have happened at all.

Call those accusations out for exactly what they are: lies, falsehoods, fabrications. The people who told you those lies weren't deliberately trying to deceive you, but they were incredibly ignorant and they did not know any better.

That's not an excuse for their corrosive behavior, but that's enough context to address the fact that you are more than enough. You are neither a mistake nor an accident. You're here for a purpose.

Your disabilities have given you hidden advantages that "normal" people do not possess – you just have to figure out what those advantages are and put them to work for you. The fact that you have picked up this book and you have made it this far into the content says so much about your inner character.

You are brave enough to confront your own weaknesses and determined enough to push through the barriers to become someone better. You care enough about yourself and your situation that you have taken the time out of your life to get the help you need. You are truly an amazing person!

Average people don't challenge themselves. They don't look for answers. They don't even acknowledge that there is anything that they can do to change things.

They settle for blaming other people because that's simultaneously less painful and less difficult than taking an honest look at yourself in the mirror and acknowledging the problems are inside of you – not your environment, not your past, not your upbringing, not your job, not your house, not your neighborhood – you.

You're not average. Just by reading this book you've put yourself on the path to greatness and you have the power to see it through to fruition.

Stop Doing What Average People Do

Average people are late. They don't pay their bills on time. They aren't reliable. They aren't accountable. They aren't trustworthy. Stop doing the things that get you lumped into being average.

Make it your goal to be above average, the kind of person who always delivers, who always goes the extra mile, who gives 110% of themselves no matter what the project is or what's required of them. Be the kind of person that people know they can trust and who holds themselves accountable for delivering what they've promised to deliver on time and better than expected.

Above average people aren't late and they pay their bills on time because they plan ahead. They have multiple different plans for how they will deliver on time, and they anticipate problems.

They think 5-6 moves ahead of every decision they make so they know exactly how they will handle things if the first plan doesn't work.

Above average people don't overcommit themselves. They don't make promises often. When they do make promises, they make sure they are more than capable of delivering.

They know how to say "no" to things so that when they do say "yes" they can show up in a big way.

Being average doesn't require planning. Being average doesn't require the discipline needed to deliver. Being average doesn't require discernment on what to say "yes" to and what to say "no" to doing.

You can say yes to anything when you're average because you know you're not going to be expected to deliver on most of it anyway. But you want to change your life, and that means you can't live like average people do anymore.

CHAPTER 4: Fuck the Excuses

"On the road to success, you can't afford excuses."

Eric Thomas

You have your reasons for why you are where you are and why you can't get out of where you are. Somebody somewhere will sympathize with you and make you feel better about those reasons, but if you want to change the situation then there's really no way to sugarcoat this: Fuck the excuses.

If Only Life Could Be That Easy

You see these entrepreneurs and celebrities buying million dollar homes and fancy new cars. You think to yourself, "If only life could be that easy," right? But how do you think they got to the point where they could make those decisions?

You're looking at the results of their refusal to accept excuses. You're seeing the fruits of the labor that got them where they currently are. You fail to recognize what that celebrity had to do to get to that point.

You don't see the hard work, the sleepless nights, the heartbreak, the loss of friends and family, or the sacrifices that led to their success.

If you want to achieve great things, you are going to have to give up your fucking excuses. Commit to your dreams and accept no defeat. Otherwise, you can just close this book now and continue living an average life.

The Only Thing That Matters Is Results

Whatever your reasons, they are not legitimate reasons. They are simply excuses in disguise. Here's how you can tell the difference: if the life of someone you loved depended on achieving that goal, your "reasons" would evaporate and you would find a way to do it. You wouldn't care what sacrifices you had to make to get it done. You would make them.

We live in a world that is driven by results. No one cares about your excuses, if you want out of the life that you've got right now, the first thing you have to sacrifice is those excuses.

They have to be eliminated from your vocabulary. You cannot speak them, you cannot think them, and most importantly of all – you cannot believe them.

They are lies that are keeping you from getting the results you so deeply desire. Success is your birth right! There is a reason that the desire for success is built into you. You were meant to have it and to achieve it, and you should not feel satisfied until you have it in your hands.

Take a moment and examine those excuses that you share anytime someone asks you why you're not pursuing that dream you mentioned years ago. You were not meant to quit in the face of life's challenges, those challenges were meant to strengthen you so that you would become the person you have to be in order to achieve your dreams.

How many times have you let those excuses steal your dreams from you? Stop letting the excuses hold you back from achieving what you were meant to achieve. Focus on getting the results you desire.

Sacrifice Is Unavoidable

You've spent most of your life trying to find a way to have your cake and eat it, too. The greatness that you desire is not going to come easily. In order to gain it, you have to be willing to sacrifice. You cannot put stipulations on what you will or won't do when you are pursuing your goals.

You must have an attitude geared towards doing whatever it takes to reach it. If you are currently unsatisfied with your situation and you want to change your life, then you must follow suit and change your life.

Change your routine. Whatever it is that you're doing now in your current life is clearly not working.

People all around you are getting the promotions they want or the abs they've talked about for years, and they're fueling their bodies with foods that will sustain them. They're starting the businesses they've always wanted, buying the new house and the new car, and getting married to the person of their dreams.

That's what they are doing, while you are sitting around not willing to do what they did to get there.

Stop now and ask yourself: what are you currently doing to get yourself in that same position?

A better question may be: what are you doing that is stopping you from getting to where you want to be?

What is it that you are holding onto that you are not willing to sacrifice in order to get where you want to go?

The Sacrifices Aren't Always What You Think They Will Be

Sometimes the sacrifices you must make in order to get where you want to be aren't what you think. Sometimes the sacrifices are pride, vanity, your concerns about what other people will think of you, your fears of failure, your worries about the future, or the identity that you've built for yourself.

If you cannot leave your ego behind and be willing to be made fun of and mocked, to be ridiculed and told that you're a dreamer, to be scoffed at and told that you should stick with what you know, then you won't get far in this journey.

Following your passions is quite a risk. People won't always see your vision. Most of them won't understand what you're trying to do, but that doesn't mean that you're wrong.

That just means that they lack the ability to see what you do. You're going to have to build it for them before they can believe in it. Beyond that, this also means that you're going to have to build your own steadfast belief in yourself and what you are capable of doing.

You're going to have to believe so strongly in your own vision that you are willing to blaze that trail to it and build it up with your own two hands regardless of what other people think or believe about you.

You're going to have to keep building it while other people are laughing, playing, or relaxing. Only you will know the true value of your vision, and if you want to see it happen, it's going to be up to you to deliver it.

Sacrificing Excuses

Excuses make it easy for you to let yourself off the hook for achieving results. You can point to the excuse and say to yourself, "If only that hadn't happened, I could have achieved what I wanted."

Sacrifice those excuses. Stop letting yourself off the hook. Hold yourself accountable for results because nothing else matters now.

Things will always come up whenever you're trying to achieve any goal. There will always be obstacles to face and challenges to overcome. Those aren't reasons to give up or quit because they make you stronger and prepare you to become the person that you'll have to be in order to get where you want to go.

Quit saying that you can't lose weight because you don't have the time to go to the gym. You think you're the only person who is busy?

Be honest with yourself. If you wanted it badly enough, you would be willing to wake up at 4 am so that you could be on the treadmill by 5 am and back home by 6:30 am to get ready before making it to the office by 8 am. Prioritize your time.

Quit saying that you can't get out of debt because you don't have enough money. Time is money. How often are you spending your time on television and stuff that doesn't pay you rather than investing that time in creating the life you want to live?

Be honest with yourself. If you really wanted out of debt, if it mattered to you as much as you say, then you would make a plan and you would be willing to make the sacrifices that it will take to get you there.

Quit saying you don't have enough. You have everything you need to get wherever it is you want to go in life. You are more than enough and you have more than enough to get what you want.

You just have to learn how to use what you have and stop wasting it. You've got a wealth of knowledge, wisdom, experience, and skills to offer the world. No more excuses.

Sacrificing Blame

It is nobody else's fault that you haven't achieved your dreams. It doesn't matter that they didn't believe in you. The truth is, if you had believed in your own vision strongly enough, it wouldn't have mattered what they thought. You would have made it happen anyway.

You may have started off life with a bad hand dealt to you, as alluded to in the previous chapter, but your choices determine the outcome of the game of life. The liberating thing about realizing that you, and you alone, are to blame for where you are is that it means no one else is responsible for your success, either.

You alone have the responsibility for building

that. It is your choices that will determine your destiny and no one else's.

As long as you keep blaming other people and your circumstances for where you are, you are holding yourself hostage to their power. You can't find solutions to your problems until you accept that you can find them and that it is your responsibility to find them. Once you've accepted responsibility and decided on a path forward, you'll find that things start opening up for you.

Sacrificing Denial

There is another big sacrifice you're going to have to make: stop living in denial. Denial is so comfortable. It doesn't require you to admit the truth or own your present circumstances.

As long as you deny that you have any problems that you need to deal with, you can keep shoveling the blame on everyone else. If only they would do such and such, then you wouldn't be where you are. Denial of the truth is the number one reason why people stay stuck.

No matter how much you want things to be otherwise, the truth is the truth. It isn't going to change for you. The sooner you accept the truth, the sooner you can get the help you need to make progress.

There's no shame in needing help from others but there is much shame in denying that you need it and continuing to fail because of something that's so easily and simply resolved by reaching out and asking for what you need.

Face up to the fears you have and own the truth about where you are. It's the only way you're going to be able to make real changes or get to the root of the things that are stopping you from succeeding.

It's time to sacrifice denial and move on with your life. You will be much happier, much healthier, and far better equipped to tackle challenges if you will stop denying that you have anything to do with creating them.

Sacrificing Comfort

You have to give up your grasp on the things in life that bring you comfort if you're ever going to succeed. Growth is not comfortable, change is not comfortable, but success never comes to you in your comfort zone.

Average people live in the comfort zone. Greatness occurs only outside of the comfort zone.

You aren't going to make greatness happen while you're sitting in your easy chair, sipping a beer, and watching sports. Nothing great will ever happen to you while you're staring at someone else who has gone out there and tackled the life of their dreams.

It isn't until you get up out of that chair and do something hard, the hardest thing you quite possibly will ever do, something you've never done before, and conquer the obstacles in front of you. Take the time to master your craft and read every single book, magazine, and guide that relates to what you are pursuing.

Be willing to put yourself out there in front of hundreds, possibly thousands of people, risking failure for the prize ahead of you even though only you can see beyond the effort. That's not comfortable, but eventually it can be.

Does that make you uncomfortable because it's new to you and you're not good at it yet? It should, because then you will find great things happening to you. If you want to be a success in anything, you absolutely must get out of your comfort zone.

You'll gain confidence along the way when you see those minds change, you'll get more and more comfortable with it, although the anxiety and fear of rejection will never completely disappear. You're going to have to endure a constant state of discomfort if you want to continue growing and achieve your goals.

CHAPTER 5: FEED Your FOCUS

"Most people have no idea of the giant capacity we can immediately command when we focus all of our resources on mastering a single area of our lives."

Tony Robbins

Achieving any goal is going to take a lot out of you. You're going to have to "feed your focus" if you want to be able to get where you are going. Your mind will crave what you continue to feed it. This chapter is going to be a guideline for what you need to do in order to FEED your FOCUS.

F.E.E.D.

F.E.E.D. is an acronym. It stands for food, exercise, education, and devotion. You are a body, mind, and soul creation. These three parts of you are indivisibly linked. What you do to one you do to the others.

You need to take care of all aspects of yourself in order to be able to achieve peak performance and to be able to obtain that level going each and every day as you strive to achieve your dreams.

Food

F represents food. Watch what you are putting into your body.

What you put into your body will determine the upper limits of what you can expect to get out of your body. If you are putting in junk, you won't be able to get the maximum limits of what your body is capable of achieving.

Think of your body as if it were a car. What you need in order for the car to work is gas (fuel). Your body uses the food (fuel) for energy.

When you put in low grade fuel, your car has to have more of it more often because most of what you're putting in is of low quality. The higher the quality, the less you'll need in quantity.

This will help with finding ways to feed your focus. It will also help you to surround yourself with things that will keep you motivated.

It will help you to push through the inevitable obstacles and achieve more than you ever thought possible simply by maintaining a well-balanced diet.

Exercise

The first **E** represents exercise. Exercise keeps the blood flowing through your body and the oxygen going to your brain.

If you're not exercising, which can be as minimal as a 15 minute walk a day, you're not getting that blood circulating and the brain isn't getting the full support it needs. You're going to feel less energetic.

You're going to get tired faster and more often. You're also going to be less alert.

In order to conserve the small amount of oxygen that you're making available to your brain, it's going to try and shut down as many processes as possible right when you're trying to maximize the output you're getting.

Exercise also releases endorphins that will help you keep a positive mental attitude. Positivity allows you to push through when the inevitable challenges come up and you are facing obstacles that seem impossible to overcome. Endorphins fuel the positivity that is the root of your success.

They will make you feel better about yourself, about your situation, and about your life. They will lead you to believe that better things are possible for you. Sustaining that belief is a crucial component of accomplishing your goals.

This means you need to get moving physically so that you can keep moving mentally.

The endorphins released won't just make you feel better about yourself and your life. They will literally improve your ability to focus and prioritize. Which, of course, is the key to getting anything accomplished at all.

Your ability to prioritize will help you make sure that you're getting things done in the most effective and efficient manner possible so that you can get more accomplished in less time – and that's a huge advantage when you're trying to avoid getting outworked.

What you do with your body is just as vital as what you feed your body. Fuel up every morning with a healthy breakfast that will give you the energy you need to get things done, then jumpstart your brain and your circulatory system by exercising. This early routine will structure how the rest of your day goes.

You'll be more energetic, more alert, and you will find it easier to prioritize and to focus on the tasks at hand. Getting your daily dose of endorphins will help you feel better about yourself and your life and will keep you feeling upbeat when you're facing obstacles and challenges.

Education

The second **E** is for education. Just as your body needs food to survive, so does your brain.

And the food that the brain needs most is information and opportunities to learn. When you read a book, multiple parts of your brain are activated. Reading causes your brain to process all of the information as if it were happening directly to you.

You suspend your natural disbelief based on your own life experiences and actively open up your mind to new possibilities. You are more likely to retain the information you've read, and to gain more out of it, once the book is finished.

Read biographies and autobiographies of people who have weathered the same challenges you are now facing. Learn how they overcame them, what strategies and techniques that they used, and what they discovered along their journey.

Don't just read information about the things you want to accomplish, although that is valuable. Many of the ideas you need to get where you want to go are going to come from sources that seem completely unrelated.

Warren Buffett, one of the wealthiest and most successful men on the planet, spends 80% of his day reading. In fact, there is not one single multi-billionaire who does not report that they spend a significant portion of their day reading books. If you think you don't have time to read, I challenge you on this.

Starting today, read one book a month. You will save more time by devoting yourself to reading than you will by expending all of your energy trying to get somewhere you've never been without help from someone who's already been there.

Devotion

The **D** represents devotion. Devotion means meditation or prayer. Devotion is to the soul what education is to the brain and food is to the body.

Spending 15 minutes a day in meditation or prayer clears the mind of all the rubbish that tends to collect overnight, calms the brain, and allows you to think more clearly. This is not speculation, but scientifically proven.

You don't need to use any specific prayer or meditation to get results. Prayer and meditation allow you to tap into your spiritual senses and the ability to connect with the creative power of the spiritual realm.

Meditation allows you to learn how to calm your body and to become centered with yourself. This makes it easier for you to control your emotions so you can resist cravings and other distractions that might tempt you away from your work.

Prayer doesn't have to be long and complex. Go to your favorite place in your home, grab a pen and paper, and write a letter. You do not have to share this with anyone so don't filter yourself.

Don't apologize for where you are in life. Just write what's in your heart and let it pour out of you. Then be prepared to listen throughout the day for a response to what you've written.

Look for ideas or opportunities that open up to

you. Keep a journal and watch the magic begin to unfold.

F.O.C.U.S.

Now that you've taken care of your body, your mind, and your soul, you are ready to get to work on your goal. Like F.E.E.D., F.O.C.U.S. is also an acronym designed to help you remember what you need to know in order to get where you want to go.

Future

Where do you want to be in one year, three years, five years, ten years? One way that can help you figure that out is to create a vision board.

Vision boards are the foundation for creating an action plan for the future you desire to obtain. It is a visual representation of your short and long term goals.

Maybe even gather some of your friends together and host a vision board party. I have vision board parties once a year and my vision board is in my bedroom so each morning when I wake up I am reminded of why I should stay focused on my goals.

Keep your eyes firmly set on that future result you want to achieve. It is important to be very clear on what you want to manifest in your life.

Let nothing distract you from it. Let nothing tempt you away from it. Set the firm and fully formed intention that you are going to have the future you strive for.

Also write a letter from your future self to your present self-describing what your life is like now that you've finally arrived. Describe how grateful you are for the struggles and the sacrifices that you made.

Describe the person you needed to become when you finally got here. Set that vision board near you in your home or work space and keep your letter with you.

Read the letter when you have spare time on your hands so you are constantly reminding yourself of where you want to go and what you want to become.

That future reality has to become so real to you that you see it happening in your dreams. The first place we practice any new habit or any new trait we are trying to adopt is in our dreams.

It happens to students learning foreign languages and to people who are trying to make changes. It's also where you'll be tempted to revert back to old habits.

Pay attention to your dreams. They are a barometer for how real you've made your vision and how much resistance there is in your brain.

Opportunity

When you have a goal, you need to have your eyes peeled for opportunities to make that goal become yours. Keep your ears and eyes open for conversations, offers, and openings that might be relevant to you.

If you see the opportunity, or you hear someone talking about it, step up and ask about it. Don't let your chance pass by without you at least taking a shot at it.

Since you never know when that opportunity might appear, you need to make sure you are always prepared for it. Keep your information and the materials that would allow you to take advantage of it within reach of you at all times.

Carry a bag of supplies that would allow you to seize any chance that comes your way. Keep a notebook and a pen handy so you can jot down names, numbers, and emails of people you meet.

There isn't a rule that says you have to wait for opportunity to come to you. Create opportunity by putting other people's eyes and ears to work for you.

Let them know what you want, what you can do, and what you are prepared to do in order to achieve your goal. Share information with them about your progress and updates. Keep those lines of communication open and flowing.

Commitment

Commitment is a scary thing for many people. You build back doors, bridges, and ways out – "just in case" you fail. And the reason you fail is because you are spending all of that energy building those back doors, bridges, and ways out rather than committing to getting what you want accomplished, done.

Think about the sunlight. When it's dispersed,

and scattered, it can heat things but it can't ignite them. When that same sunlight is focused into a single energy beam by the power of a magnifying glass, it becomes a laser.

That laser can start a fire, cut through solid steel, cause water to boil, and melt the hardest substances. It becomes a powerful weapon for accomplishing whatever it is that someone wants to wants to achieve.

Your commitment is the magnifying glass that will focus the rays of your energy into a laser point. It sets your heart and your mind to work on finding answers to any and every problem, obstacle, or block that you might face.

When you are truly committed to your vision, you will ignite the minds and the hearts of the people around you and you will get them moving with you. Commit to the goal and the means to make it happen will come to you.

Undefeatable

This is the word you need to apply to yourself from now on in terms of your goal. You are going to be undefeatable. No matter what comes your way, no matter what obstacle stands between you and your goal, you are undefeatable.

Life can't stop you, disease can't stop you, even death can't stop you. You are not going to be defeated no matter what happens.

As part of your undefeatable mentality, you know you must adopt the "fuck the excuses" mindset. You can't accept any excuse. If they build a wall between you and your goal, you're going to tunnel under that wall or catch a plane and parachute on the other side of it.

If they put you in a locked cage, you're going to learn how to pick the lock. Nothing will stop you. Nothing on earth can hold you back. This is yours. You've got this.

If you fail to achieve it the first time, you're not going to go home with your head hanging low and your shoulders slumped. You're going to pick yourself back up, examine what you did wrong, figure out a new path forward, and try again.

You are never again going to let a loss or a failure be the excuse you use as to why you didn't do something. You're going to do it. You just haven't done it yet.

Sacrifice

In chapter four, we already discussed the need to sacrifice in order to achieve your goals. Whatever does not bring you closer to achieving your goals, whatever does not support you in getting done the things you need to do in order to get what you want, that is something you need to lose.

Provided that you have chosen a worthwhile goal in the first place, let nothing and no one stand in your way.

If you discover that you invest too much time into social media, and that is time that could be spent working toward your goal, then social media has go! Delete the apps off of your phone, temporarily, and stay focused.

If you are tempted by television, sacrifice it. Unplug it out of the wall, remove the batteries from the remote, and hide them away.

Make setting everything back up so difficult that it would take more time to put it back together than it would to use it. Force yourself to think about what you are doing and why.

If you are edging toward obsession with your emails, schedule a time to check them once a day but then stay away from them.

Whatever it is that steals your time, your energy, or your opportunities – sacrifice it. Sacrifice the bad habits and the bad attitudes, also.

The money you are spending to support bad habits can be put toward achieving your dreams.

The attitude you are sporting that is driving people away is preventing you from making the connections you need to be successful. Sacrifice it.

Achieving your goals is going to require a head-to-toe, inside-out transformation of yourself.

Now That You Know It, Apply It!

None of this information is going to get you any closer to your goals if you don't apply it. Don't read this book and then put it down and let it collect dust. Your life won't change that way. I want you to experience the benefits, but that won't happen until you apply what you've learned.

Just by picking up this book and reading this far, you've already put yourself in a class ahead of others. It was a declaration to yourself that you have a dream and a goal, and that you don't know how to make it happen.

Because you are in a class ahead of others, I'm going to challenge you to do more than they do. Don't just read it. Don't just absorb it. Apply it!

Each and every day, FEED Your FOCUS. Put the things into your mind, body, and soul that will support you in putting in your maximum effort each and every day. Don't quit until you get there.

This journey is going to push you to the limits of

what you think you are capable of doing and it will be demanding. Don't worry. You have what it takes. I know you do.

CHAPTER 6: Develop A Strong Work Ethic

"And where I excel
is ridiculous,
sickening, work ethic.

You know, while the
other guy's sleeping?

I'm working."

Will Smith

There is much confusion and misunderstanding in modern society regarding the true meaning and appearance of a strong work ethic. When I think about the people in my life that have embodied this ideal to the fullest extent, my grandfather comes to mind.

He would work very long hours in order to provide for my family, but he was able to put in the work because he knew the value of taking care of his family. He was more than willing to do whatever was required of him so that he could keep food on our table and clothes on our backs.

That was the main goal in his life, and it fueled him to never stop. And a life like my grandfather's is the living definition of a strong work ethic. His time, his energy, and ultimately his health was sacrificed for the goal set before him; he valued our family so highly that he refused to to let anything outwork him or tear him away from us.

Developing a strong work ethic is not about merely setting a goal or having a few ideas in mind of what you want to achieve.

It comes from knowing why you set those goals in the first place. Why are your goals worth all of the effort, the sacrifice, the time, the money, and the energy that you're going to have to give up in order to achieve them? Why are they worth facing your biggest fears and risking failure, ridicule, and hardship?

The average person has no idea what the value of achieving their goal is because they've never taken the time to think about it. Because of this, when push comes to shove, they're willing to let it go too quickly. Why are you driven?

If you don't know why you're fighting for something in the first place, you won't fight for it when things get tough. Weak-willed people pick goals that lack any real meaning or achievement because they don't genuinely value the transformation that comes from achieving real goals.

They don't value change because they've never stopped to think through their motives and purpose. You will not be the weak-willed person floating through life with no apparent passion.

You are going to know – and own – the value of your goal. Spend ten minutes with a pen and paper to fully answer that question for yourself.

Right now. Grab some sticky notes. Get to work with reminders of your mission statement, your purpose, and your goal. Then, place those anywhere you can that you know you'll see everyday, multiple times a day: your mirror, your windshield, your computer monitor, wherever.

Do not waste the time or the opportunity that you have now because they will not always be here waiting for you. Sit down and spend ten minutes of your time listing out all of the reasons why you want that goal, knowing that it will change your life when you do get it.

Remind yourself constantly of what achieving your goal will bring you and why that matters.

Work Doesn't End Until the Daily Goal Is Met

Take that big, terrifying, incredible goal that you've set for yourself and break it down into smaller, easier-to-achieve goals. Then, take it a step further and turn those smaller, easier-to-achieve goals into things that you are willing to do each and every day to start working in the direction that you want to go.

This is the key to the next part of developing a strong work ethic: Work does not end until the daily goal is met.

If you have twelve hundred miles between yourself and your goal and you could only walk for a single mile each day, then your work day should not end until you have walked that single mile. It may take you twelve hundred days (just under four years) to get there, but you will get there.

Should you take your time, or let yourself become overwhelmed by the idea that your goal won't come quickly, then you're just prolonging the time it will take you to get there.

But by breaking your big goals into smaller, measurable goals and believing that your work does not end until that goal is met, you will make great progress toward your goal.

Savor that progress because progress in itself is its own achievement. Achievements are rewards that encourage your brain to keep going and keep working. At first, you'll need those rewards of progress to get you motivated, but you will quickly become addicted to the feeling.

These are real, tangible achievements that you can point to. Every single one that you accomplish adds to the list of things that you know you are capable of doing.

Every time you add to that list of things that you are capable of doing, it builds your ability to sustain your belief in yourself. It increases your confidence and sense of assurance. Self-confidence is the greatest indicator of whether or not you will achieve what you set your mind to.

Work Hard, Play Harder

As you develop a strong work ethic, your mind will begin to transform, learning that hard work results in getting to play hard when the job is done. Train your brain to adapt to this reward system by setting small rewards for achieving your daily goals.

For example, give yourself ten minutes of something you enjoy that you've sacrificed up until now to achieve your goal – and even bigger rewards for major milestones.

If you include rewards for your loved ones along with rewards for yourself, this will make it easier for your loved ones to be patient while you're working toward your goals and will also give them a reason to cheer you on as you go.

Imagine it this way: if a child is promised a trip to Disney World on the condition that he or she keeps their grades up for the semester then you'd better believe that child will be turning in their homework and studying for their tests all semester long.

If that kid really wants to go, then they will not have poor excuses for why they couldn't take care of their responsibilities.

The only way you'll get to go on that trip, to achieve your dream, is if you make results along the way, and those results won't come if you put in the hard work that's necessary.

Planning time to celebrate the small victories

and recognize your achievements along the way will keep your brain motivated to stay on track.

It allows you to feel good about what you've done while at the same time giving you something to look forward to when you're navigating the various obstacles and hurdles that come up throughout your journey. Ultimately every effort spent, every achievement celebrated, it's all part of developing a strong work ethic.

Stay Productive, Not Busy

There's a great difference between busy work and productive work. Busy work is done with no endgame in mind, lacking a purpose.

It's the kind of work that gives you something to show for the time you've spent but it does nothing to help get you any closer to where you'd want to be after you've finished it.

On the other hand, productive work is meaningful as it gives you a measure of how much closer to your goal that you've come once you've completed it. No matter what, stay productive, not merely busy.

When working toward a goal, every step taken should be done with that goal in mind. It does not matter the time or the place; if you're at a social gathering and networking then be listening for how you can work with other driven individuals to help you achieve your goals while helping them to achieve theirs at the same time.

If you've got down time at home, be planning and researching. You're always on the clock, always working toward your goal, and always productive. This doesn't mean that you're physically working all the time, otherwise you'd exhaust yourself.

Both your brain and your body need time to recharge and replenish. You will get much more done and be far more productive if you're intentional with your time to rest and to rejuvenate yourself.

It is when you are not doing anything meaningful that your brain has time to sort through all the information you have collected and find the relationships between the unrelated bits. This is where the most inspiration comes from and why it so often happens to you in the shower, when you're dreaming, or when you're driving.

Put Off Procrastination

If it needs to be done, get it done now, no excuses. If you're going to put off doing anything, put off procrastinating. Procrastination is the number one reason that people get outworked – and sadly it's the most preventable of all reasons.

Remember this: every time you choose to procrastinate taking care of a piece of work that you know you need to take care of in order to get where you want to be, you are putting your dreams on hold. You are giving someone else the chance to come in and steal the opportunity away from you.

Everyone has responsibilities that they cannot stand, it doesn't matter who you are. If you're able to, consider delegating those tasks to someone else who can take care of them for you. If necessary, pay a little to be done with those responsibilities so that you're freed up to focus on your goals. This may be hard for some who want to do everything for themselves, but it isn't necessary to be an expert in everything.

Choose someone who finds joy in that kind of work and let them go at it. If you can't delegate those tasks, ask yourself if they're absolutely necessary. If the answer is yes – then get them done first thing rather than putting them off for later when you're less likely to do them. By choosing to do them first, you earn a stress-free day without having to worry about the tasks you dread. You can then focus on doing what you enjoy for the rest of the day and make progress with ease.

If the reason for your procrastination is that you don't know how, or that you lack sufficient information to take steps forward, then get busy learning and equip yourself with the intellectual resources that you need to achieve your goals.

Go out and ask someone informed and experienced for advice on what you should be doing and when. Get online and do some research. Find a relevant book that will educate you. Stop telling yourself, "I don't know how," and go figure it out.

Be Grateful

A strong work ethic is about much more than just working. It's how you show up each and every day to work. If you step back and think of your work as something beneath you, or as unnecessary, then you're going to resent it at some point or another.

You're going to constantly fight it because you see it as below you and an injustice that you should have to exert the energy at all. A hard worker knows that there is no work beneath them when committed to a single goal.

Every ounce of work that it takes to get the job done gets you one step closer to where you want to be and you should be grateful for each and every step of the journey. That lack of gratitude is going to cause you to overlook and miss out on major opportunities in life.

Imagine the following scenario: two men are

assigned the exact same job cleaning out stalls in a horse barn. It's backbreaking menial labor, the job never changes, and the work stinks – literally.

One man hates his job. He daydreams of a better life and he feels this work is beneath him. He shows up every day with a surly attitude and looks for every opportunity that he can find to get out of doing his share. He's miserable because he believes for a fact that nothing good will come out of this job and the job will never change.

He begs for other work but he keeps getting turned down, largely due to his horrible attitude, though he's oblivious to that fact. Even though he's capable of doing a great deal more than what he's currently doing, nobody is willing to trust more important work to him because he can't seem to handle this menial work well.

The second man is extremely grateful for the job. It may be menial labor, but it provides for his family, and he values that far more than his own ego.

He comes into work each day with a smile on his face, knowing that each time he shovels out the manure, he's getting his family a little closer to where they want to be in life. One day, he notices some plants growing amid the manure piles that are healthier and taller than the other weeds. He gets an idea and goes to his boss.

This man asks his boss for permission to bag up the manure that he's shoveling and, on his own time, sell it to the neighboring farmers. He promises his boss that he will give him a quarter of any profit he makes by doing this. His boss admires the plan and agrees to it.

As a result, this second man begins working two additional hours after work each night to sell the manure to the farmers as fertilizer. They're grateful for his work ethic, his boss is making more money because of him, and the man feels even happier about his position because he knows that every shovelful of manure is like a step closer to securing his family's well-being.

In time, the boss sees the success of the plan and promotes the second man to manager of the stable crew. The boss knows that no matter what he puts this man in charge of, the man will work diligently to ensure it prospers.

As the manure business is going strong, this grateful man is able to hire his own salesmen and save himself those extra hours he would spend by paying them a percentage of the profits.

In just over a year, each of the two men's lives have totally transformed. The first man's surly attitude and lack of willingness to work eventually gets him fired.

He finds getting another job even more difficult than the first one because of the reputation he's created for himself. Nobody wants him because they know he's an unpleasant person to be around who will avoid work as much as possible.

But the second man's grateful attitude has seen him achieve several promotions and build his own successful business. He's now able to achieve goals that people used to laugh at him for believing were possible – and his attitude was instrumental in making that happen.

No matter what work is given to you to do, no matter how menial you believe the labor to be, approach it with gratitude. Know that opportunity is found in every problem. If you can solve that problem for yourself, you can solve it for someone else. You can trade your knowledge and skill for whatever you want.

Look For What Needs To Be Done & Do It

Here is another major area where people far too often miss out on opportunities to shine: waiting to be told what needs to be done. It's one thing if you're new to the job and unsure of your duties, still exploring the policies and procedures of your employer.

However, once you know your job well enough to know what needs to be done and how to do it, then take the initiative. People will notice and your hard work will pay off.

I have a friend who worked in a fast food restaurant. This was not where she wanted to be in life, but she was grateful for the job because it allowed for her to provide for her family.

Every time she walked through the doors, she made it a point to look for what needed to be done and made sure that she was the one out there doing it, regardless of being asked or told to do so.

Eventually, this got the attention of the store manager. He'd never seen a work ethic like this. He appreciated her efforts and subsequently offered her a promotion even though she'd only been on the job for a few months – all because of her work ethic.

This attitude of taking the initiative will set you apart from everyone else who only does what other people tell them to do. It is the hallmark of true leadership.

Apply this same attitude not only to your work life, but to your home life, and to being a citizen of the area in which you live. See what kind of a difference you'll begin to make. If more people would adopt this simple change in attitude, many of the world's problems would be solved in record time.

CHAPTER 7: Create A Plan

"By failing to prepare,
you are preparing to fail"

Benjamin Franklin

Trying to achieve a goal without creating a plan of action just doesn't work. It's not logical.

Imagine you want to drive to New York City for the first time. You hop into your car and just start driving with no map and no concept of how long it will take to get there. You have no plan. Do you believe you'll make it to NYC?

Maybe, but it's not likely. You might end up in the right place, but you're far more likely to end up lost and wondering what went wrong. If you're serious about your goal, get serious about creating a plan to achieve that goal.

Be Clear About What You Want

Clarity about what you want to achieve needs to mirror that of a GPS. A starting pointing, an ending location, and a route on how to get to where you are going. Without it how will you know when you've gotten there?

Your goal should be clear enough that you could explain it to a child and they would be able to understand it. You don't have to have every detail correct, but the more details you can include in your plan the more likely you are to get what you want out of your efforts.

For example, setting a goal of owning a house

is good. It's a place to begin. But you need to ask yourself what kind of house you want? How many bedrooms? How many bathrooms? What features would you like to have? In what neighborhood would you want that house to be located?

Once you have these details, you can take that vision and go research the rest of the information you will need in order to create a more concrete plan to get that house and make it your reality.

Know Why You Want It

What you want out of life holds great value but what is even more valuable is knowing why you want what you want. If you don't know why you are doing something, you'll never finish.

Knowing why is the key to keeping you motivated until the end.

Knowing why you want to achieve a goal often determines what resources you're going to need and affects the timeline for getting it done.

For example, it's one thing if that trip to New York is just a personal desire of yours and has no impact on your life as opposed to needing that trip to New York in order to attend your aunt's funeral.

The personal desire trip doesn't have anything other than a self-imposed deadline. You can take as long as you want to get there. The funeral trip has a definitive deadline and an expiration date for the plans.

The costs are going to be higher for the funeral trip, depending on how quickly you have to be there, which means you are going to need more resources than you would for your personal trip.

Your reasons matter when you're trying to recruit help to get your task done. People are more inclined to help you get somewhere if helping you benefits them in some way or if they see your goal as being one that they can empathize with and would want help in similar circumstances.

For example, if they know that the reason you have set a goal of going to New York is because you have six months to live and this is on your bucket list, you're far more likely to find people willing to chip in and support you on seeing that dream become a reality.

However, if they know that you are set to go to a funeral in New York for your Aunt but only hold great interest because she was filthy rich and promised to give a percentage of her money to every person who made it there, they aren't likely to be motivated to help you unless there's some kind of payoff involved in it for them.

Having a reason that speaks to other people's

dreams and desires makes it easier to get them cooperating with you in achieving the goal, and that makes it more likely for you to actually achieve that goal.

Know Why You Want It

Deadlines determine costs. That's true when you're booking transportation, flights and hotels, and it is true in many other areas of life. The sooner you want it, the higher the price you're going to have to pay to get it. Keep that in mind when you are deciding to set the "when" portion of your goal.

Knowing when you want to achieve your goal is the key to being able to take the resources you'll need to acquire and break them down into measurable, actionable steps forward each day that will take you steadily forward toward achieving that goal.

This isn't just in reference to the amount of money. It's also in reference to the amount of work you're going to have to invest in achieving that goal.

If you are trying to write a 60,000 word book, you only have to write 600 words a day in order to finish that book in 100 days. However, if you want to finish that same book in 30 days, you must write 2,000 words a day.

It takes a very slow writer 1 minute to write 10

words, so 60 minutes to write 600 words. It's much easier to find one hour in a day than it is to find the 200 minutes (or 3 hours and 20 minutes) to write 2,000 words.

You may need to readjust your timeline, if you can, after assessing the resources you have to achieve your goal. If the "when" can't be adjusted, you'll need to get creative with your resources in order to meet your needs.

Know The Value of Achieving It

What is achieving this goal worth to you? This is an important question to ask yourself because you're going to be investing a lot of your time, energy, and resources into gaining it. You want to be sure that you are investing in something that is worthwhile and will bring you long-lasting benefits.

Assess the goal in terms of four areas of living: physical, mental, emotional, and spiritual health. What is the current monthly cost of living the way you are living right now? How much do you spend each month in doctor's bills, in pharmaceutical purchases, or in lost wages due to time that you have to take off of work to deal with your health issues? Multiply that monthly number by 12.

How much time do you spend depressed, anxious,

or worried? If you were getting paid by the hour for that time, how much would it add up to?

Now imagine a life where you weren't living the way you are now. Imagine a month where you weren't concerned about what bills came in because you knew there would be money in the bank to cover them. Imagine not having to live under a cloud of stress, anxiety, depression, worry, or fear. What would that life be worth to you?

Imagine being able to take off whenever you wanted to in order to go and explore the world around you? What would that life be worth to you? Write down that number and add it to part one of the value.

Write these things down and keep them in front of you. Remind yourself of this value when you are feeling resistance to doing what you must do in order to achieve those goals.

Assess Your Needs

What are you going to need in order to achieve your goal? Sit down for 10 minutes and brainstorm all the things you are going to need in order to get where you want to be.

If you were taking that trip to New York, this is the point where you start writing things down like "transportation, lodging, food, spending money, clothing."

The needs assessment is important for multiple reasons. This is where you sit down with the fears you have about getting where you want to go and you let fear speak up and tell you all of the things that it sees as potential dangers to your health, happiness, or safety.

Listening to fear is the best way to get over it. Once you've heard fear out, you can create solid plans that will allow you to overcome any obstacle that may come up along the way.

Fear is not there to hurt you or to get in your way. Fear is there to warn you, and if you listen to it, it will be a huge help to you in creating the plan. It spots all the potential problem areas, the pitfalls and the areas where things can go terribly wrong.

The mistake most people make is in trying to shoo fear away without listening to it. They want fear to shut up. So, take the time to let fear speak and tell you all about what you are going to need to overcome in order to get where you want to be.

Assess Your Resources

Now that you know what you need, it's time to assess what you have in terms of resources that you can use. Your resources fall into five key areas that I will explain later: knowledge, skills, time, connections, and tangible resources. Each of these can contribute to meeting the needs that you have, especially if they are leveraged creatively.

Knowledge

Knowledge is priceless and it can be traded to get assets you need to achieve your goal. Sit down with a pen and paper and spend 10 minutes brainstorming all of the things that you know. Don't discount anything.

Don't discard the information you have as irrelevant or unimportant. It may seem trivial to you, but it may be the exact thing someone else needs to learn in order to solve a problem they are currently experiencing.

Skills

Skills are all the things you know how to do. Like knowledge, it is priceless and can be traded to get what you need. As you did with knowledge, spend another 10 minutes with pen and paper brainstorming everything you know how to do no matter how trivial you may think it is.

Quite often, we take for granted those things that are easy for us to do because they seem like no big deal to us while other people would pay a premium for help in doing that exact thing.

Time

Take a close look at how much time you have to invest in achieving your goals each day. You can't make more time, but you can use your time more efficiently. If you have to spend 9 hours of each day at work and you have a 1 hour commute each way, that only leaves you 7 waking hours each day to spend on your goal.

Take away the time you need to do your morning routine, FEED Your FOCUS, and the time you need to cultivate relationships with your loved ones, and you may only have 2 hours a day to spend on your goals. Keep that in mind when determining how quickly you want to achieve your goal.

Connections

One of the most valuable resources that people have, and the one that is the most often overlooked, neglected, and abused, are the connections you've formed with other people. Everything you want to create or achieve is going to require other people to help you get there.

To figure out what resources you have available to you, make a list of all the people that you know and all the things that you know they can do or that they can access. Reach out to those people and find out what their goals are.

Create a plan that takes you one step closer to your goal by helping them get closer to their goals. People are more likely to cooperate with you in achieving your dreams if they can see how helping you achieve your dreams will get them closer to achieving their own.

Tangible Assets

What are the physical possessions you own and the monetary resources you can access that you can leverage to buy the help you need or acquire the resources you don't have that will get you closer to achieving your goal?

Make a list of those and, when you're done, see who on your list of connections might be willing to trade what you have to get what they need so that it becomes a win-win for both of you.

Fill In the Gaps

Once you've gathered your prepared list of resources, look over the list of needs. What gaps are there between what you have and what you need? This comparison of what you have to what you need can be eye opening. Don't let it intimidate you. When the needs list seems to exceed that "already have" list, it's not impossible to achieve your goals. It's just going to take creating a concrete plan that builds you toward the things you need to get or being creative with the resources you do have to get more of what you need.

Take a look at your connections. If you've already started contacting them and finding out their goals, it becomes easier to figure out how to get what you need. You look at what you have left over that you don't need to achieve your goal. You see what you have that matches up with what they want or need to achieve that goal.

You also look at what they have that might match up with what someone else on your list wants or needs. Then you create a plan that allows you to trade what you have for what someone else on your list wants or needs in order to get from them the things you need to make your plan happen.

Filling in these gaps does sometimes require

that you be willing to sacrifice things you've been holding onto in order to create room for what you want in your life. That can be difficult and feel uncomfortable. However, you have to decide what is more valuable to you: the thing you've been holding onto or the goal you desire.

Be honest with yourself about that, and make your decisions accordingly. Otherwise, you may gain what you need but you'll end up resenting the person you obtained it from or the things you gained. You may feel they forced you to do something you didn't want to have to do. You'll poison your own success with resentment and anger.

Break Down the Steps

Now that you know where the gaps are and what you need to achieve your goal, break down the big goal into smaller, bite sized daily chunks. Let's say that you need to raise $2.5 million dollars and you have just 5 months to get that done.

Talking about raising $2.5 million dollars without having a plan on how you are going to do it is daunting. Breaking that down into smaller, bite-sized chunks makes the goal manageable and feel more attainable.

This means that you need to raise $500,000 per

month, or $25,000 per day assuming you work 20 days out of a 30 day month. You look at your assets and you realize you don't have a product or a service you can offer others that people would be willing to pay $25,000 in order to obtain.

However, after talking to a few of your contacts and connections, you discover that your friend has a friend that is willing to teach people how to sell a product for $10,000 that will make you $5,000 every time you sell one of them. If you can sell 5 of those a day, you can hit your target.

That's why you need to break down the steps into achievable, believable chunks. You can have anything you want in life if you can visualize yourself getting it. Creating a plan provides clarity towards making it happen. Breaking the steps down goes a long way toward making the big goal feel more reasonable and possible.

It is a lot like plotting a course on a map. You know how close you are getting to your goal by checking to see which milestones you've passed along the way. For example, if you're travelling from Texas to New York you know you're headed in the right direction when you cross the state line into Arkansas, and you know you're getting much closer when you pass through Washington D.C.

Create the Vision

When you are climbing up a mountain, you're exhausted and the pack you're carrying seems far too heavy for you to go even one more step. It's natural for your brain to tell you that what you are doing is crazy and you should quit. It's natural for your brain to tell you this isn't worth the pain, the struggle, and the suffering.

You're literally unable to see the campsite and the beauty of what you're going to attain because you aren't there yet. If you quit now, you will never get to experience the joy of it. Having the vision in front of you reminds you of what it is you are working to gain and why it is worth it.

The vision board is something I recommended earlier. Create the vision board for your end goal, but then create a visual road map that leads you to it.

Every time you achieve something that brings you closer to your end goal, move the "car" a little bit closer to your end goal. Not only does this help you to stay on track, but it allows you to visually see your progress.

There are many times when you will feel discouraged or struggle to achieve something. You need not only the big prize at the end but the tangible reminders of progress along the way. Creating the road map does that for you.

It reminds you that even if you may be stuck in the slow lane right now or even if traffic happens to be stalled on the highway, you're still making progress. It is a way of encouraging yourself to continue by reminding yourself of just how far you've come and by reassuring your exhausted, tired, beaten up body that the end is just ahead.

Get Feedback On Your Plan

This step is something I highly recommend, but it needs to be done carefully. You don't want feedback from just anyone. You need feedback on your plan from someone who has already been where you want to go. That kind of feedback is invaluable.

Going back to the mountain climbing analogy, someone who has never climbed the mountain you are preparing to climb may know in theory what you need. But they don't have the hands-on experience that of someone who has actually done this will.

They don't know the terrain and where the bridges tend to wash out or where the rockslides are most likely to happen. They can't give you specific tips or shortcuts that can make your trail easier.

Once you've created that plan, take it to people who have already done what you have done or something similar to it and ask them for their feedback. Ask them to give your plan a review and to tell you what you are missing or what you can dump in order to accomplish your vision.

Such feedback might require an investment, but the investment you make in gaining that feedback will be well worth the time you save or the trouble you bypass by getting it.

CHAPTER 8: Be Obedient To The Vision

"Champions aren´t made in the gyms. Champions are made from something they have deep inside them - a desire, a dream, a vision."

Muhammad Ali

When you have a vision, or a dream, or a goal, you might think that it belongs to you and that it is yours to do with as you see fit. That's an amateur mistake. Your vision, dream, and goal are not yours.

They are far bigger than you. You are simply the person they have chosen to help transform them into reality.

Before I speak about obedience to your vision, I want to throw out some cautionary notes so that you're not deceived later on. If you're stranded in the desert and you're completely lost, you're likely to encounter two things: an authentic vision of water coming from an oasis up ahead and shimmering mirages that promise what they cannot deliver.

The wise traveler learns to distinguish between the two so that he's not led astray, possibly to his death, following the shimmering mirage.

Before you decide to give yourself over in obedience to anything, you need to be sure that what you are dealing with is an authentic vision rather than a shimmering mirage.

An authentic vision gives you hope that is based on the truth and will, therefore, never fail to deliver. It will only disappoint you if you have false expectations about reality.

As long as you're living in alignment with the truth, it won't disappoint you or lead you astray.

An Authentic Vision Versus a Shimmering Mirage

A shimmering mirage promises to deliver your heart's desire but it is a trap that leads you to utter destruction. A shimmering mirage is based on false hope, constructed out of ego, and paved with pride.

It satisfies you in the beginning but ultimately leaves you empty, hopeless, alone, and afraid. It will lead you into denial of the truth and beat you up for believing its own falsehoods.

Test your visions before you pursue them. Authentic visions and shimmering mirages both require sacrifice to gain. Authentic visions require personal sacrifice and your own blood, sweat, and tears to accomplish.

No authentic vision will be easy to reach. Anything that is truly worth possessing will require something of equal value from you.

These shimmering mirages promise to give you everything without you having to sacrifice anything of your own but they are false glimpses of hope.

If the shimmering mirage requires a sacrifice, it is of something that isn't yours to give up in the first place. It promises to give you something of great value without requiring anything of yours in return. Beware of giving into shimmering mirages.

Service Is the Hallmark of An Authentic Vision

I can guarantee you that any authentic vision will not be self-serving. You'll receive rewards for achieving that vision, but those rewards are not the vision's end in itself. An authentic vision exists to serve the world and the people who occupy that world, plain and simply.

Close your eyes and imagine the time when your vision has come to fruition. Who is being served by this? Whose life is being improved by the achievement of this vision? How, exactly, did achieving this vision help them?

If you can't honestly say that anyone other than you benefits from this vision, then it's not genuine; it's far from an authentic vision and you should be careful about pursuing it.

It is a shimmering mirage that will end up leading you in the wrong direction and you will find neither joy nor fulfillment should you continue following that path.

Love Is the Fulfillment of Any Authentic Vision

If the vision is authentic, then it will pull you away from relationships that are unhealthy for you. Instead, it will push you to cultivate and develop those relationships that are leading you toward love. Love is the ultimate fulfilment of any authentic vision.

If your vision makes you more patient, kinder, more forgiving, gentler, slower to anger, increases your compassion, your generosity, and so on, then this is a genuine vision worthy of pursuit.

An authentic vision will not steal time away from your children, your spouse, or your family, nor will it force you to choose between it and the important things in life. It will help you incorporate them into your vision and make serving them a part of your plan.

If your vision seems to insist that you should isolate yourself, if it encourages you to cut people out of your life to make progress, if it asks you to sacrifice time that you should be spending with your family, then it is not an authentic vision. It's a counterfeit.

Many have sacrificed every relationship that they had to achieve wealth, power, privilege, or material gain. They sold themselves to this false notion believing the lie that it was the only way to get what they wanted.

They made no time for family or friends and, when they reached the heights that they had set out for, they discovered that what they had spent their life building was empty and meaningless without people to celebrate it with them.

It didn't satisfy. There was no one to enjoy their success with them and not a soul cared about them or their achievements.

The few friends that are now at their side lack an ounce of loyalty in their entire character. There was always an air of doubt in their mind about why some people stayed or why they were liked at all.

A small part of them never stopped whispering that if they didn't have the success or the money or them to the side hoping to return to them when you've finished building whatever it is that you wish to build, do not expect them to be waiting for you when you're ready to go back to them.

That's unfair and not how relationships thrive. They're growing and changing just like you, their lives are unfolding with or without your presence, that's a face you'll have to accept.

Though they may want you in their lives, they will eventually learn to live without you. When you build, be sure that you are including them in the process. That way they will still be there when the building is done and you'll have genuine friends to celebrate the new life that you've created.

Let Your Vision Lead You

As soon as you take action for your vision, you'll quickly discover that it takes on a life of its own. No matter how careful and detailed your plans, they will be absolutely dismantled once they meet reality. You'll need to let go of the original plan and be prepared to revise as circumstances change.

Trying to force your vision to obey your plans is the best way to destroy your chances of seeing that vision enter reality. In fact, that's what causes a vision to stop speaking to you altogether.

Trust your vision: let it lead you. Trust that it is there to guide you toward good things, and listen to it when it tells you what you need to be doing and when.

Be obedient to the vision. You've never in your life been where that vision is trying to take you.

You don't know the road that lies ahead nor are you aware of the pitfalls and the traps that are along your way. But your vision does; it's been to the future and it lives there. It knows how to navigate the terrain.

That vision came to you not because you were the most qualified person for the job nor because you were ready for it. It came to you solely because you were open to obeying it.

You allowed it to whisper its promises in your ear and share its story with you. You entertained that vision and made it welcome in your mind. You believed in it and it gave you its trust in return.

Do not ruin that incredibly valuable trust by ignoring it. Don't weigh that vision down by putting the burden of your expectations for how it should behave or what it should look like on its shoulders.

Remember, you don't own your vision. It is a partner. The minute you try to control it, it will stop cooperating with you and start fighting you.

This is not because it is angry or spiteful, it's because it's trying to stop you from making mistakes. You're going to slow down the both of you by increasing the amount of work it has to do in order to guide you to where the two of you need to be.

Now, you may fear letting go of the illusion of control over your vision, perhaps thinking that it will result in the vision leaving you. However, that vision doesn't want to abandon you.

It chose you for a reason and never would have

sought you out if it didn't see your potential to see it through. You are uniquely qualified to help it become a reality: your vision needs you, just as you need it.

The only thing that you can do to destroy the vision or make it flee you is to try and control it. If you allow it to go the direction that it wants to go and you let it tell you what work to do and when, you will find that what manifests itself is infinitely greater and more powerful than you could ever have imagined on your own.

CHAPTER 9: Accomplish Your Goals

"I can't relate to lazy people.
We don't speak the same language.
I don't understand you.
I don't want to understand you."

Kobe Bryant

You have a big vision and the goals to support it. You know why you want those goals, when you want to achieve them, and the value of making them happen. You FEED your FOCUS daily, and you are obedient to your vision. Here are five ways that will guarantee you accomplish your goals.

1. Create Your Own Mixtape

Before the days of iPods and Spotify, when I wanted to win the heart of a girl, I would make her a mixtape. I would select songs that would remind me of her in some way and that communicated my vision of the two of us together. I put them on a tape or CD, and then gave it to her so that she could hear my voice speaking to her through those songs.

I didn't want her to forget me, or to stop thinking about the two of us being together, and music was the means of guaranteeing it.

Do the same thing for yourself and your vision. Create your own playlist of motivational speeches and inspirational songs that keep you energized and aware of what you're working toward.

For example, I start my day off by listening

to Les Brown, Eric Thomas, Tony Robbins, and Zig Ziglar. You may listen to completely different speakers or music artists.

Whatever motivates you, find it and feed off of it everyday. Listen to it each and every morning and throughout the day. Let it remind you of the reasons you're chasing your goal.

Get yourself fired up and ready to go back out there, pumped up and eager to fight for what you want. Encourage yourself daily, stay motivated to push through difficulty because it is far too easy to give up when you become frustrated.

In this day and age, everyone seeks instant results. We live in a time where we have unlimited amounts of information at our disposal in a matter of seconds with the advent of smartphones, Google, and more.

Within a minute, we're reading an article that provides the exact answers we were seeking. Our curiosity is satisfied almost without effort.

In light of this, it follows that we expect similar 'instant results' in other areas of our lives. And yet, as anyone knows, life does not work like a search engine.

We tend to get discouraged when we fail to see the scale move instantly after we've worked out for a couple of days consistently or studied a subject diligently. In a culture of fast-food convenience and immediacy like no other society has known before, we tend to want similar overnight results when we're working towards our fitness goals.

In your quest for instant gratification, you'll find many shortcuts, but I urge you not to take them. These shortcuts may satisfy your urges for a short time, but in the long run you're only doing damage to your mentality.

Growth requires patience. Train your brain to believe that big goals come with hard work.

You must put in the work, the hours, and the sleepless nights. You have to make the sacrifices. When things get rough and results fail to come as quickly as you'd like, do not give up!

Push harder. Give more than you gave when you started, push harder than you've done before, let your passion take you places that you've never imagined.

You don't have to pretend that it will be easy, but when you're scrolling through your social media, don't envy the people that have followed their passions and created incredible lives for themselves. Know that they didn't do it without putting in the time and effort.

You see them and it may make you feel like all of your efforts are failing you but never is that true. Never compare yourself to others. Always keep in mind that building anything worthwhile takes hard work. Don't forget that everyone has to start somewhere.

Whenever I'm feeling discouraged or down, I listen to my mixtape and I get myself charged back up and in the right mentality, ready to face the world and conquer. Winners have down times, too, we just don't let them keep us down.

We find ways to pick ourselves back up and get out there faster than the average person. And your mixtape is a very helpful tool to achieving this.

2. Be Willing to Change

Change is inevitable. You are going to change whether you want to or not. The only choices that you have are how you change and whether or not the changes you are making will improve you or damage you.

When working toward accomplishing your goals, your vision is going to push you to change.

A lot. You will stretch and grow to become an entirely new person if you're ever going to reach the lofty heights where your vision sits.

It will not be comfortable or easy, you must accept that. There are days that this new life you're living will feel completely foreign. You might feel unlike yourself, but this is because you are building a new you.

You are not the same you that existed before you picked up this book. You've changed already. You're going to have to adapt to the new you that you are becoming.

Do not sit idly by waiting for change to happen to you. Go out there and pursue it. Don't resist the change, become it. Look forward to the opportunities that open you up.

One thing about change, though, is that you can't expect it to happen in an instant. It's very normal for your body and your mind to resist the change. You have to have the willpower to supersede the resistance. You've spent a lifetime developing habits that will not disappear overnight. You will have to actively, consistently, and consciously work at them.

It won't be easy – especially in the beginning – but it will be worth it. Change, by definition, requires your brain to remap your neural pathways. That is energy that you mind does not, by default, like to spend if it doesn't have to. You'll have to take charge of maintaining the new, better habits you are forming as you are working to change into the person you must become to achieve your of your goals.

Don't forget to go easy on yourself, at times. If you have a day or two where you're unsure of what to do, beating yourself up isn't the answer. Pick yourself back up, make a firm resolution to do better next time, and get back on the path before you.

Forgive yourself and forget about it. Continuing to beat yourself up will only result in giving up on your new habits before you ever hit your goal.

3. Don't You Quit

Life lesson: you will never be closer to achieving the thing you desire most in life than on the day that you are ready to quit and give up.

The bigger and more ambitious your goal, the more that life will test you to be sure that you are worthy of achieving it.

Visions have power to transform the world

for good or for evil, and that much power must never fall into the hands of one who is not truly prepared to use it.

"Good things come to those who believe, better things come to those who are patient, and the best things come to those who don't give up."

Zig Ziglar

Life will test you. It will tempt you to quit, it will discourage you, it will make you doubt yourself. If you're facing discouragement and are down in the corner of your room, curled up in a ball, wondering why you're doing this to yourself, it's time to take that why statement back out and remind yourself why this vision matters.

It's time to take the focus off of your own pain and remember all of the lives that will be changed by your success. Those people need you, the world needs you, and they need you now.

They need you to keep going toward what you aimed for from the beginning and finish strong.

4.   Learn from Failure

You're human, don't forget that. You're trying something new with your life and you will experience failure from time to time, if not frequently.

Sometimes you'll miss the mark, sometimes the ball won't make it in the hoop, but you shouldn't quit on yourself or give up on your vision. You need to study what you did wrong and learn from it.

Every failure has a lesson to teach you, but you must be willing to own your mistakes and learn from them. The fool refuses to acknowledge the lesson, he keeps on repeating his errors.

The wise man accepts the consequences and

refuses to be caught by the same mistake twice. Be wise: learn from your failures and don't repeat them.

Nobody starts life off succeeding at each and everything they do, everybody drops the ball eventually. You didn't walk out of the womb ready to give a speech or run a marathon. You had to learn to talk and walk.

You failed plenty of times before you managed to succeed at either of those things, but you accomplished all that and much, much more.

Failure means nothing beyond the fact that you're still learning how to do what you want to get done.

5. Be Prepared

Don't just show up, show up ready to work. Show up with all of your gear and be ready to get the job done. Show up mentally, physically, spiritually, and emotionally prepared.

If you're working toward a fitness goal then you need to be prepared to eat the right food in the right proportions and to eat consistently throughout the day so that you aren't hungry for long periods of time.

When you're prepared, you're ready to do the right things at the right times and to do them consistently so that you can achieve the results you want. Always be prepared.

Prepare what you need the day before so that you aren't wasting time and energy trying to find what you need in the moment, potentially forgetting something important. If you're tempted to take the easy route, fight the urge and trust that the longer route is better for you in the end.

I follow this principle in maintaining my fitness goals. I cook all of my meals in advance, so typically I'll cook 3-4 days' worth of meals at a time.

Because of this preparation, I don't have to wonder what I'm going to eat when the time comes or run to the grocery store at the last minute.

I'm not tempted to stop and eat foods that I know are detrimental to my goals. That preparation means I don't go shopping when I'm hungry, which is where many fail and purchase items that have no place in their kitchens.

This mentality applies to much more than just material items. It's just as important to mentally prepare yourself. I like to expect certain outcomes in various situations. I think about what could go right and how I plan to build from it.

I'm also prepared to bounce back from whatever may go wrong. When certain things happen, I'm not surprised or caught with my tail between my legs.

Instead, I'm able to remain calm, collected, and strong because I've already anticipated the outcome. This is what mentally prepares me for every situation.

Find Accountability Partners

This is crucial. When you're all alone with only the thoughts in your own head, it's very easy to get down and excuse yourself from pushing as hard as you could.

It's also much tougher to resist temptation when facing something that you know you don't need to be eating when you don't have anyone you're going to have to answer to.

Don't fight alone. Find an accountability partner who will help you in these situations.

Make sure that your partner is someone working toward a similar goal as you and who is just as committed to seeing you succeed as you are. Choose someone who is an encourager but who won't hesitate to tell you when you're off track.

It feels good when others can witness the changes that you are making and go through the journey with you so that you can provide support for them as well.

If your partner works with you, then they will be the deterrent you need to resist the temptations to quit, give up, or indulge yourself.

Better yet, if your partner lives with you, then they will see your habits and deter you from sliding back into unhealthy, unproductive ways that will tear you away from your desired goals. Together, the two of you can work as a team to get more accomplished than either of you could alone!

Social media makes it easier than ever to find accountability partners. There are many Facebook groups that are free to join that offer support for almost any goal you could want to set. Join them, get to know the people in there.

If you don't like the atmosphere of a group, hunt for one where you feel comfortable and welcomed and then engage it frequently.

Set weekly check-ins with your partner.

Knowing that you're going to have to give hard numbers and provide facts helps you stay on track because you know that you're going to have to be honest if you haven't done it. Make sure that you're working with someone you like and trust, but who is not going to let things slide.

It's important that your accountability partner is working toward the same goal as you because then you can't bullshit them and tell them that they don't understand your struggle or your pain.

They do, and you know it, because they're right there in the trenches with you. They've either been through it already or are facing it currently, and they're not giving up so neither should you. You both know that, so it eliminates the excuses before you can even get them out.

Track Your Journey

The easiest way to battle discouragement and fight the temptation to quit is to remind yourself of your successes. That can't happen, though, if you aren't tracking them.

Keep a daily journal of your progress. See how much further you can get today than you could a few weeks ago.

There is nothing more encouraging than looking back at old pictures of myself and compare them to where I am now. I can easily see how far that I've come and how much more that I'm capable of today.

I can physically see the growth and the improvement which reminds me that even if I'm not seeing improvement today, continuing to apply myself will result in even greater improvement in the time to come.

If you haven't been tracking your own journey, start today. Set a deliberate intention to record every step you take toward making that goal a reality.

This way, when you look back, you'll be able to see just how far you have come and you'll be encouraged to continue. It also makes it easier for your accountability partner to see what you've been up to and point out the progress that you've made.

CHAPTER 10: Finish Strong

"Success isn't owned - it's leased. And rent is due every day. Every single day, someone's coming for your job. Someone's coming for your greatness. If you're the greatest, someone wants to be the greatest, and so if you're not constantly improving your game, somebody else is."

J. J. Watt

Throughout our lives, and especially while we are working hard to achieve a goal, opportunities will come our way.

Some will be great and some won't be worth your time. A crucial part of finishing strong is knowing when and what to say no to while pursuing a goal.

Know When To Say No

Always trust your gut. If you are proposed with an opportunity of any sort and you feel unsure, unexcited, and unpassionate, you should take all of those feelings for what they're worth. It's a no!

If something is really for you, you will know right away. You will feel some form of excitement and maybe have ideas of your own to add.

That initial moment of hesitation is one big red flag. If you lack passion, it is very likely that you will not see the project through. Never start something you don't think you will finish.

If you feel as if you are starting and stopping projects constantly take that as a hint that you are taking on things that you should have never started in the first place.

You don't want to be known as a great starter

but a poor finisher. Without realizing it you could be giving yourself that reputation right now if you don't know when to say no.

Say yes to the things that align with your vision and your passions. Say yes to the things you love.

Say yes to the things that add value to the world. Say yes to your passion.

It's important to know when to say yes as well, because sometimes our vision can lead us to unknown territory. You'll know when to say yes, when you feel that inkling of hope and excitement.

Push Yourself Harder Than Ever

The "Don't Get Outworked" mentality is very difficult to put into practice. It helps me to think of life and its difficulties like a work out, and it may help you to do so as well.

When you're almost done with your routine, you can either cruise by or you can push harder. You should always push harder. One more rep, one more mile, whatever it takes to push through.

No matter what I am doing, I work very hard to finish strong. I push myself that extra little bit right at the end, so that I don't just cross the finish line, I blow past it. When you do only what is required of you, you teach your brain that you can get by without going all in or giving it everything you've got.

That mentality can be very damaging, especially when life places you in situations that are much more difficult than just running a race or lifting some weights. You must train yourself to think tough, and be tough.

Test your abilities and your strength. When you feel like giving up, but instead you give every last ounce of everything you've got, I promise you will be pleasantly surprised.

You'll be shocked to see what you are truly capable of when you push yourself beyond that point. Your full potential does not lie in a comfort zone, so push through that comfort zone into unknown territory.

That is where your full potential awaits you; in the unknown. It is important to finish strong no matter what.

Treat Every Task With The Same Sense of Purpose

Whatever you put into the little things in life is what you will put into the bigger things in life. I believe this to be very true.

We often say, "Oh well, that is not important. If it was a bigger deal then of course I would try harder," but when push comes to shove, we do not.

The individual who approaches every task, big or little, easy or hard, with the same sense of purpose and drive to better than they were yesterday, along with the determination to finish strong, will always outwork the individual who only tries when they want to.

Consistency is key in training your brain to adopt a new mindset or approach to life. I strive every day to be a person of this resolve, and it is very difficult in a world full of fast food, easy decisions, convenience, and instant gratification, but I still do it. More importantly, YOU CAN DO IT!

Our culture is full of get-rich-quick-schemes and lose-weight-by-barely-trying lies and they want you to believe that you can give the smallest amount of effort and achieve your goals. This is simply wrong.

You have to work hard. You have to make sacrifices. You have to stay consistent. You have to feed your brain. You have to make wise decisions. You have to fight with all of your heart and finish strong.

When I'm required to complete a small, trivial task, I still give it one 110% because I know that when the time comes for me to do something that really matters, I will do it to the best of my ability.

I want to be the person whose second nature is to finish the job strong, to not even have to think or question whether or not I am going to do it. Until that point in my life, I will not stop.

Heed the Advice

This advice may fall on deaf ears, so to speak, because you may have heard similar statements or stories and you may have written them off for a variety of reasons. Maybe you're hoping you will hear something else someday that will knock you out of your laziness.

Maybe you are perfectly content with just getting by and don't care about finishing strong because you don't think it matters.

Whatever the reason may be that you are choosing to ignore the advice, I understand. People get numb to motivational stories and inspirational quotes about finishing strong and giving it your all.

You may think it's just a bunch of hype and that it doesn't matter, but based on my experience, it matters. I have personally witnessed the difference between the people that are content with just getting by and those who choose to finish strong.

Heeding the words of others who have come to their conclusions the hard way and learned from difficult experiences is wise. I know it's tough to keep these things memorable and meaningful. Facebook, Instagram, and Twitter bombard you with a ton of different inspirational articles and memes every single day.

This can numb you to the point where none of it really means anything anymore because you've seen the same thing day after day, several times a day.

That doesn't change my advice. I still tell you finish strong because that is what is best for you, for the people you love, and for the jobs you agreed to do in the first place.

It is what is best for your reputation and for the changes you are trying to make in your life. It is what is best for your vision and for your goals.

Compete with Yourself

If you take nothing else away from this book, I want you to remember this: work harder than you did yesterday, finish strong, and compete with yourself.

Don't settle for yesterday's best. Push past that to achieve more than you've ever achieved before.

One of the greatest errors I see people making is comparing themselves to others without factoring in all of the time, effort, opportunity, and other things that went into making that person who they are.

People just say, "I want to be the next Steve Jobs" or "I want to be the next Michael Jordan" and then are surprised when it takes more than an overnight workout session or a week's worth of effort to get there. Comparing yourself to others will only drive you to disappointment and discouragement.

Compete only with yourself. This will prevent you from setting unfair standards. It gives you a level playing field against your competition. Only you can be the best you.

These statements may sound obvious, but so many people forget that becoming the best at anything in the world starts by pushing yourself to be the best you can personally be.

You might want to be NBA level by next year or be able to lift three times your body weight in a couple of months. Those goals aren't necessarily wise or realistic. It depends on your personal level of fitness as to how realistic and achievable they are.

However, you can and should always set a goal to do better today than you did yesterday. Do one more rep, one more lap, one more stretch, one more of whatever it was you did yesterday.

Set your goals a little higher than the day before and don't let yourself quit until you reach them.

Pace Yourself

Finishing strong requires you to learn to pace yourself so that you don't burn out all of your energy and focus at the beginning. If you burn out, you'll end up doing the exact opposite of what you set out to do.

It's foolishness, plain and simple. Life is a marathon, and running a marathon isn't about speed. It's about endurance.

The best marathon runners know that the key to success is achieving that steady rhythm of moving ever closer to your goal until you are right up on the finish line so that you still have more energy left to give, and then giving it all you've got in that last tenth of a mile.

They know that pacing yourself means always pushing through, never giving up, and finishing strong no matter what the cost.

It's time for you to get out there and run that race. It's time for you to strive toward your dreams and stop telling yourself you can't. It's time for you to decide that you aren't going to get outworked ever again.

And I'll be right here, cheering you along, holding you accountable for your results.

Sincerely,

Darren Taylor

ABOUT THE AUTHOR: Darren Taylor

Darren Taylor is an author, business owner, fitness model, father, mentor, and long-time entrepreneur. His passion lies within motivating others to reach their full potential. Everything Darren has achieved can be attributed to his fool - proof work ethic. Throughout Darren's journey he has learned that success requires sacrifice.

He realized in his self-development that he had to remove every person, habit, and self-defeating thought that would hinder his success. Every day, Darren reminds himself that time is our most precious commodity, and he refuses to waste any of it on "broke activities." He has never had a goal that he hasn't achieved because he maintains laser focus on them.

Darren is compelled to share his story, his motivation, and his work ethic with anyone who has a desire to change their life as well. Allow his story to increase your own self-awareness by identifying your weaknesses, excuses, and toxic relationships.

Connect with Darren Online:
INSTAGRAM
@dontgetoutworked
FACEBOOK
http://facebook.com/dtaylor214
WEBSITE
http://www.dontgetoutworked.com

RECOMMENDED READING: My Personal Favorites

Think and Grow Rich by Napoleon Hill
See You At The Top by Zig Ziglar
The Alchemist by Paulo Coelho
Extreme Ownership by Jocko Willink and Leif Babin
The War of Art by Steven Pressfield
As a Man Thinketh by James Allen
Who Moved My Cheese by Spencer Johnson
Outliers by Malcolm Gladwell
The Magic of Thinking Big by David J. Schwartz
Tribes: We Need You to Lead Us by Seth Godin

CPSIA information can be obtained
at www.ICGtesting.com
Printed in the USA
FSOW03n2045290417
33610FS